Spot the Shape

# Shapes in Sports

## Rebecca Rissman

Heinemann Library
Chicago, Illinois

© 2009 Heinemann Library
an imprint of Capstone Global Library, LLC
Chicago, Illinois

Customer Service: 888-454-2279

Visit our website at www.heinemannraintree.com

Designed by Joanna Hinton-Malivoire
Photo research by Tracy Cummins and Heather Mauldin
Color Reproduction by Dot Gradtions Ltd, UK
Printed and bound by South China Printing Company Ltd

13 12 11 10 09
10 9 8 7 6 5 4 3 2 1

**Library of Congress Cataloging-in-Publication Data**
Rissman, Rebecca.
Shapes in sports / Rebecca Rissman.
p. cm. -- (Spot the shape!)
Includes bibliographical references and index.
ISBN 978-1-4329-2170-5 (hc) -- ISBN 978-1-4329-2176-7 (pb)  1.  Shapes--Juvenile literature.  I. Title.
QA445.5.R5726 2008
516'.15--dc22
                              2008043208

**Acknowledgments**
The author and publishers are grateful to the following for permission to reproduce copyright material: ©Alamy pp. **4** (Barrie Rokeach), **11** (SBP), **12** (SBP); ©Getty Images pp. **7** (David Madison), **8** (David Madison), **13** (Debra McClinton), **14** (Debra McClinton), **15** (Dugald Bremner), **16** (Dugald Bremner), **17** (Doug Pensinger), **18** (David Madison), **19** (Stockbyte), **20** (Stockbyte), **23** (Dugald Bremner); ©Jupiter Images pp. **9** (Corbis), **10** (Corbis); ©Shutterstock pp. **6** (Saniphoto), **21** (Jonathan Larsen).

Cover photograph of a soccer ball on a field reproduced with permission of ©Superstock/Corbis. Back cover photograph of a bicycle reproduced with permission of ©Getty Images (Stockbyte).

Every effort has been made to contact copyright holders of any material reproduced in this book. Any omissions will be rectified in subsequent printings if notice is given to the publisher.

# Contents

# Shapes

Shapes are all around us.

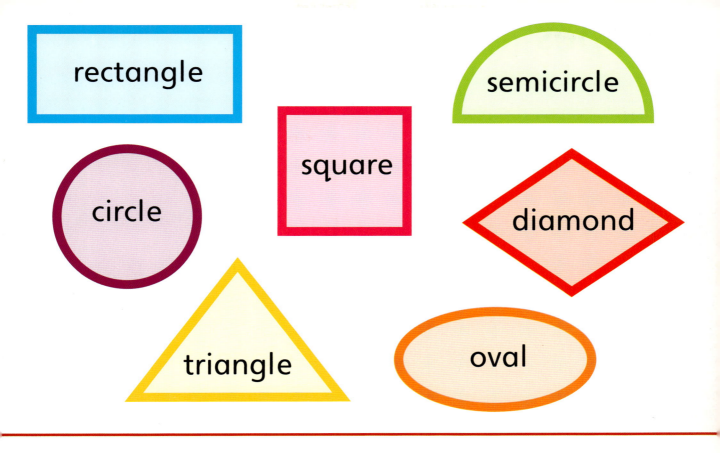

Each shape has a name.

# Shapes in Sports

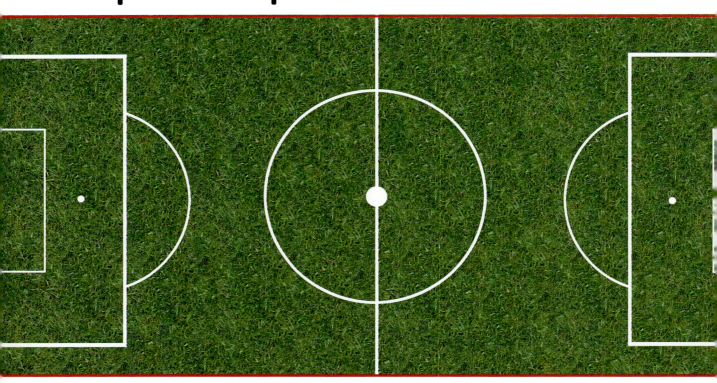

There are many shapes in sports.

What shapes can you see in these flags?

Squares are in these flags.

What shape is this sandpit?

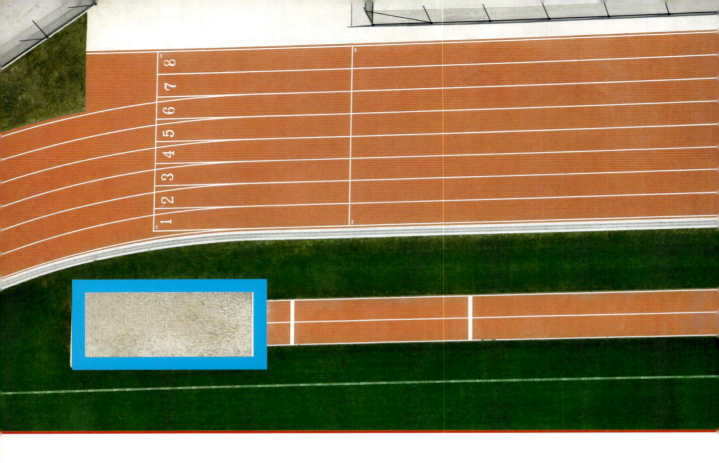

This sandpit is a rectangle.

What shape is this ball?

This ball is an oval.

What shape is this person making?

This person is making a triangle.

What shape is this kayak?

This kayak is a diamond.

What shape is on this ice?

A semicircle is on this ice.

What shape are the wheels on this bike?

The wheels on this bike are circles.

There are many shapes in sports.
What shapes can you see?

# Naming Shapes

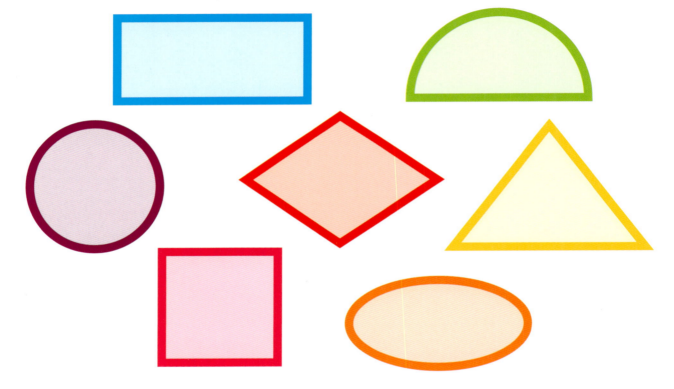

Can you remember the names
of these shapes?

# Picture Glossary

**kayak**  a type of boat for one person

# Index

**Note to Parents and Teachers**

**Before reading**
Create a simple memory game for children by drawing or pasting shapes onto small index cards. Turn the cards over and challenge children to find pairs of shapes by remembering where each shape is.

**After reading**
Miming sports: show children a variety of balls, such as a Ping-Pong ball, a golf ball, a tennis ball, a soccer ball, and a basketball. Ask them what shape you would have if you traced around the outside of each ball. Ask a child to mime using one of the balls in a sport. Challenge the other children to guess the sport.